TOSEL®
READING SERIES

READING

PRE-STARTER

2

 International TOSEL Committee

CONTENTS

BROCHURES   4

About TOSEL   4

TOSEL Level Chart   6

Evaluation   8

CHAPTER 1. In My Classroom   10

UNIT 1   A Happy Art Class   11

UNIT 2   In Math Class   19

UNIT 3   How Taki Studies   27

UNIT 4   The Class Rules   35

CHAPTER REVIEW   43

CHAPTER 2. My Day at School 44

UNIT 5   Josef's Morning 45

UNIT 6   A School Festival 53

UNIT 7   A Busy Year 61

UNIT 8   Four Seasons 69

CHAPTER REVIEW 77

CHAPTER 3. At School 78

UNIT 9   Olaf's Day 79

UNIT 10   Shopping with Your Family 87

UNIT 11   Henry and His Bike 95

UNIT 12   Tennis and Table Tennis 103

CHAPTER REVIEW 111

ANSWERS 112

About TOSEL®

TOSEL (Test of Skills in the English Language) was developed to meet the demand for a more effective assessment of English as a foreign language for learners from specific cultural settings.

TOSEL evaluates and certifies the proficiency levels of English learners, from the age of 4 through adulthood, along with academic and job performance results.

Background

- Other English tests are ineffective in accurately measuring individual abilities
- Overuse of US-dominated testing systems in diverse cultural and educational contexts in the global English language learning market

Functions & Usage

- Assessment is categorized into 7 levels
- Used as a qualification for academic excellence for school admissions
- Used as a test to assess the English proficiency in the corporate and public sectors

Goals

- Create an effective tool for assessing and evaluating the English skills of English language learners
- Implement efficient and accessible testing systems and methods
- Provide constructive and developmental English education guidance

TOSEL® Strength

LEVELED ASSESSMENTS

An established English test system fit for seven different levels according to learners' cognitive development

ACCURATE DIAGNOSIS

A systematic and scientific diagnosis of learners' English proficiency

EXTENSIVE MATERIALS

Supplementary materials to help learners in an EFL environment to prepare for TOSEL and improve their proficiency

SUFFICIENT DATA

Content for each level developed by using data accumulated from more than 2,000,000 TOSEL test takers delegated at 15,000 schools and academies

CLASSIFIED AREAS OF INTELLIGENCE

Content designed to foster and expand the strengths of each student, categorized by the eight areas of intelligence

CONTINUITY

A complete course of English education ranging from kindergarten, elementary school, middle school, high schoool, and up to adults.

HIGH RELIABILITY

A high reliability level (Cronbach's alpha: .904 for elementary school students / .864 for university students) proven by several studies (Oxford University / Modern Language Journal)

SYSTEMATIC & EFFECTIVE ENGLISH EDUCATION

Accurate diagnosis and extensive materials which provide a step-by-step development in English learning, according to the quality of each learner's ability

TOSEL® Level Chart

Seven Separate Assessments

TOSEL divides the test into seven stages, by considering the test takers' cognitive levels, according to different ages. Unlike other assessments based on only one level, TOSEL includes separate assessments for preschool, elementary school, middle school, high school students, and for adults, which also includes both professionals and college students.

TOSEL's reporting system highlights the strengths and weaknesses of each test taker and suggests areas for further development.

COCOON

Suitable for children aged 4-6 (pre-schoolers)

The first step in the TOSEL system, the test is composed of colorful designs and interesting questions to interest young learners and to put them at ease.

Pre-STARTER

Suitable for children aged 7-8 (1st-2nd grades of elementary school)

Evaluates the ability to comprehend simple vocabulary, conversations, and sentences.

STARTER

Suitable for children aged 9-10 (3rd-4th grades of elementary school)

Evaluates the ability to comprehend short sentences and conversations related to everyday situations or topics.

BASIC

Suitable for children aged 11-12 (5th–6th grades of elementary school)

Evaluates the ability to communicate about personal information, daily activities, future plans, and past experiences in written and spoken language.

JUNIOR

Suitable for middle school students

Evaluates the ability to comprehend short paragraphs, practical texts, and speech covering general topics and to participate in simple daily conversations.

HIGH JUNIOR

Suitable for high school students

Evaluates the ability to use English fluently, accurately, and effectively on a wide range of social and academic subjects, as well as the ability to use sentences with a variety of complex structures.

ADVANCED

Suitable for university students and adults

Evaluates the ability to use practical English required for a job or work environment, as well as the ability to use and understand English at the university level.

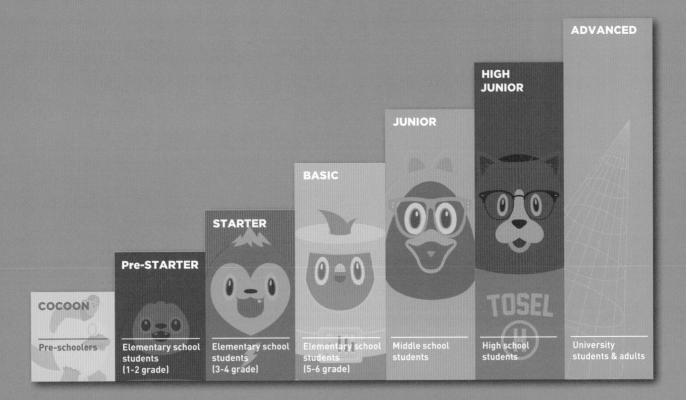

Evaluation

Assessing the Four Skills

TOSEL evaluates the four language skills: reading, listening, speaking and writing, through indirect and direct assessment items.

This system of evaluation is part of a concerted effort to break away from materials geared solely toward grammar and reading-oriented education.

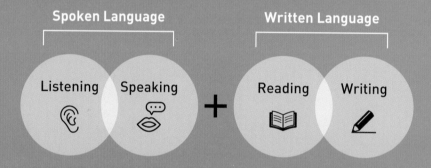

TOSEL Test Information

Level	Score	Grade	Section	
			Section I Listening & Speaking	Section II Reading & Writing
COCOON	100		15 Questions / 15 min	15 Questions / 15 min
Pre-STARTER	100		15 Questions / 15 min	20 Questions / 25 min
STARTER	100		20 Questions / 15 min	20 Questions / 25 min
BASIC	100	1-10	30 Questions / 20 min	30 Questions / 30 min
JUNIOR	100		30 Questions / 20 min	30 Questions / 30 min
HIGH JUNIOR	100		30 Questions / 25 min	35 Questions / 35 min
ADVANCED	990		70 Questions / 45 min	70 Questions / 55 min

Certificates

TOSEL Certificate

The International TOSEL Committee officially evaluates and certifies the level of English proficiency of English learners from the age of 4 to adults.

Certified by

Mar. 2010   Korea University

Dec. 2009   The Korean Society of Speech Science

Dec. 2009   The Korea Association of Foreign Language Education

Nov. 2009   The Applied Linguistics Association of Korea

Oct. 2009   The Pan Korea English Teachers Association

CHAPTER 1

In My Classroom

UNIT 1   A Happy Art Class   11

UNIT 2   In Math Class   19

UNIT 3   How Taki Studies   27

UNIT 4   The Class Rules   35

CHAPTER REVIEW   43

UNIT 1

A Happy Art Class

Teacher's Book
p.90

What can you draw?
Let's draw something!

Mila likes to go to school. She sees her favorite teacher, Mr. Shu. Mr. Shu is an art teacher. He is very kind. And he draws really well. Today the class draws flowers. At first, Mila can't draw well. But Mr. Shu helps her. Mila draws a beautiful flower garden. She is happy.

New Words

art

draw

teacher

class

Part A. Spell the Words

1.

dra_

(A)　w

(B)　x

(C)　y

2.

(A)　treache

(B)　teeachr

(C)　teacher

Part B. Situational Writing

3.

Mr. Shu is Mila's _____ teacher.

(A)　art

(B)　math

(C)　English

4.

It is a _____ garden.

(A)　rock

(B)　flower

(C)　vegetable

5. Look at the board. What goes here: _____?

    (A) her

    (B) she

    (C) she is

6. What is NOT true?

    (A) It is a math class.

    (B) There are six students.

    (C) The teacher stands by the board.

Part D. General Reading and Retelling

> Mila likes to go to school. She sees her favorite teacher, Mr. Shu. Mr. Shu is an art teacher. He is very kind. And he draws really well. Today the class draws flowers. At first, Mila can't draw well. But Mr. Shu helps her. Mila draws a beautiful flower garden. She is happy.

7. What is the best title?

   (A) Mila's Father
   (B) Mr. Shu's Garden
   (C) A Happy Art Class

8. What does Mila draw today?

   (A) a forest
   (B) a garden
   (C) a teacher

9. Who is Mr. Shu?

   (A) an art teacher
   (B) a math teacher
   (C) a science teacher

10. What is NOT true about Mila?

   (A) She likes school.
   (B) She is sad in art class.
   (C) She has an art class today.

Listening Practice

 Listen and write.

  MP3 PS2-1

A Happy Art Class

Mila likes to go to school. She sees her favorite _____¹_____,

Mr. Shu. Mr. Shu is an __²__ teacher. He is

very kind. And he __³__ really well. Today the

__⁴__ draws flowers. At first, Mila can't draw well.

But Mr. Shu helps her. Mila draws a beautiful flower garden.

She is happy.

Word Bank

teacher	class
draws	art
at	ticher
duraws	crass

 Listen. Pause. Say each sentence.

  MP3 PS2-1G

Writing Practice

 Write the words.

1
| a | | |

2
| d | | | |

3
| t | | | | | | r |

4
| | | | | s |

 Write the words.

Summary

Mr. Shu is Mila's _____ teacher. He is very kind

and he draws very well. He helps Mila.

Word Puzzle

C	O	G	M	S	Q	F	Z	C	T	H	K	O	A	S
J	Z	W	M	Y	Z	Q	I	L	H	P	E	C	N	E
M	Z	Q	O	R	U	Y	B	A	B	D	F	M	O	J
L	B	C	A	L	G	E	F	S	O	T	R	K	I	O
L	K	W	Q	N	V	J	D	S	Y	A	W	B	Q	A
O	B	R	T	D	N	J	C	R	M	O	K	G	A	R
L	L	W	S	H	X	U	O	U	F	W	G	U	N	G
I	W	L	C	H	L	U	P	O	J	H	D	Z	L	M
G	S	W	R	S	L	J	P	Q	V	Z	U	E	A	F
N	Z	W	F	N	Q	U	R	T	F	U	M	B	Z	L
S	M	A	D	K	R	P	U	H	R	F	D	A	R	T
R	P	N	H	Q	T	D	R	A	W	E	P	I	Q	F
J	Y	V	H	P	M	E	P	I	L	C	G	T	V	G
C	R	Z	H	U	X	I	V	S	B	R	V	P	G	M
Q	Z	J	T	E	A	C	H	E	R	F	I	X	U	E

 Write the words. Then find them in the puzzle.

1 _____   2 _____   3 _____   4 _____

UNIT 2

Teacher's Book
p.93

In Math Class

What do you bring to math class?
Do you like math class?

The math class starts. The teacher stands by the board. There are numbers on the board. Jason has a pencil. He has a book. He has an eraser. He puts them on his desk. He writes some numbers. But the numbers are wrong. Jason uses his eraser. Soon the bell rings. It is 12 o'clock. It is lunch time!

New Words

stand

write

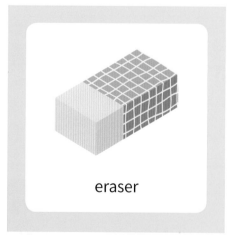

eraser

pencil

Part A. Spell the Words

1.

(A) stand

(B) stnda

(C) satnd

2.

_raser

(A) a

(B) e

(C) i

Part B. Situational Writing

3.

There is a _____ on his desk.

(A) pen

(B) pencil

(C) puppy

4.

Jason _____ numbers.

(A) paints

(B) writes

(C) erases

5.   What is the girl doing?

(A) taking a photo

(B) holding a pencil

(C) erasing a picture

6.   What is on the desk?

(A) two cups

(B) a red ball

(C) a blue book

Part D. General Reading and Retelling

The math class starts. The teacher stands by the board. There are numbers on the board. Jason has a pencil. He has a book. He has an eraser. He puts them on his desk. He writes some numbers. But the numbers are wrong. Jason uses his eraser. Soon the bell rings. It is 12 o'clock. It is lunch time!

7. Where is Jason?

(A) in a bedroom
(B) in a classroom
(C) in a living room

8. What does Jason study?

(A) art
(B) math
(C) music

9. What is NOT on Jason's desk?

(A) a pencil
(B) an eraser
(C) an orange

10. When does Jason have lunch?

(A) at ten
(B) at eleven
(C) at twelve

Listening Practice

🦻 Listen and write.

MP3 PS2-2

In Math Class

The math class starts. The teacher [1] _____ by the board. There are numbers on the board. Jason has a

[2] _____ . He has a book. He has an [3] _____ . He puts them on his desk. He [4] _____ some numbers. But the numbers are wrong. Jason uses his eraser. Soon the bell rings. It is 12 o'clock. It is lunch time!

Word Bank

stends	writes
iraser	eraser
rites	pencil
pincil	stands

🗣 Listen. Pause. Say each sentence.

MP3 PS2-2G

Writing Practice

 Write the words.

1

s			

2

			t	

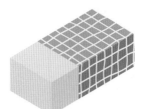

3

	r			

4

p				

 Write the words.

Summary

The _____ class starts. The teacher writes

numbers on the board. Jason writes numbers, too.

Q	W	R	I	T	E	U	F	X	U	N	W	Z	B	N
X	T	V	O	D	A	X	D	D	J	O	Z	K	Q	B
D	B	G	M	K	N	J	U	H	T	L	N	G	P	Y
U	C	W	C	G	P	S	Q	L	X	I	L	A	Q	I
P	D	N	H	E	R	A	S	E	R	W	M	T	C	H
L	L	L	X	A	U	E	X	F	K	X	G	S	G	H
A	L	I	P	W	I	S	J	Q	V	M	D	W	M	S
E	L	C	F	V	G	Q	N	L	S	E	P	X	Y	J
A	O	X	K	D	V	I	R	R	L	B	S	H	O	G
D	G	B	Q	C	W	N	S	Y	S	T	A	N	D	S
H	P	K	Y	Y	M	X	Y	N	M	X	N	T	G	D
X	A	N	X	Z	L	P	E	N	C	I	L	M	N	L
C	N	M	Y	A	A	B	V	Y	B	C	L	Z	G	N
E	J	H	G	W	W	G	D	L	N	Z	B	N	O	E
N	A	W	V	Y	F	H	Y	S	Q	E	L	M	G	L

🔍 Write the words. Then find them in the puzzle.

   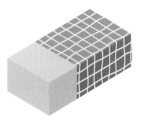 

1 _____ 2 _____ 3 _____ 4 _____

Teacher's Book
p.96

UNIT 3

How Taki Studies

What new English word do you know?
Draw it.

Taki studies Spanish. How does he study it? He reads. And he listens to music. He tries new ways. Sometimes he says the words. But he is not too noisy. Sometimes he makes songs from Spanish words. Then he sings the songs. Sometimes he watches Spanish video! Taki likes learning Spanish.

New Words

read

listen

sing

study

Part A. Spell the Words

1.

_ing

(A)   r

(B)   s

(C)   t

2.

(A)   red

(B)   read

(C)   bead

Part B. Situational Writing

3.

I _____ to music.

(A)   run

(B)   sleep

(C)   listen

4.

The guitar is _____.

(A)   wet

(B)   pink

(C)   noisy

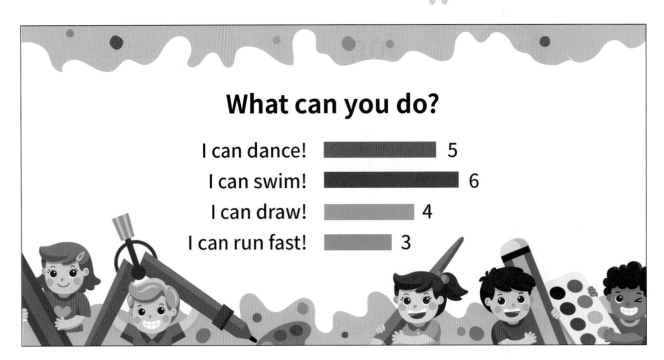

5. How many students can draw?

   (A) 3

   (B) 4

   (C) 5

6. What is true about this graph?

   (A) 5 students can swim.

   (B) 6 students can dance.

   (C) 3 students can run fast.

Part D. General Reading and Retelling

Taki studies Spanish. How does he study it? He reads. And he listens to music. He tries new ways. Sometimes he says the words. But he is not too noisy. Sometimes he makes songs from Spanish words. Then he sings the songs. Sometimes he watches Spanish video! Taki likes learning Spanish.

7. What is the main idea?

(A) how Taki sings
(B) how Taki draws
(C) how Taki studies

8. What does Taki NOT do?

(A) run
(B) sing
(C) watch

9. What does Taki sing?

(A) Korean songs
(B) science words
(C) Spanish words

10. What does Taki like?

(A) running in Spain
(B) learning Spanish
(C) eating Spanish food

Listening Practice

 Listen and write.

  MP3 PS2-3

How Taki Studies

Taki ¹ _____ Spanish. How does he study it? He

² _____ . And he ³ _____ to music. He tries new

ways. Sometimes he says the words. But he is not too noisy.

Sometimes he makes songs from Spanish words. Then he

⁴ _____ the songs. Sometimes he watches Spanish

video! Taki likes learning Spanish.

Word Bank

sings	listens
leads	stadies
signs	studies
reads	rissens

 Listen. Pause. Say each sentence.

  MP3 PS2-3G

Writing Practice

 Write the words.

1
| | | | d |

2
| | i | | | |

3
| s | | | |

4
| s | | | |

 Write the words.

Summary

Taki likes _____ing Spanish. He reads, listens

to music, sings, and speaks Spanish words.

Word Puzzle

S	Y	R	Z	P	Q	H	K	T	Q	O	U	A	A	P
T	G	O	E	Z	A	U	M	R	V	W	W	M	O	Q
U	F	H	E	F	Y	L	F	Z	U	H	X	S	N	O
D	D	X	D	F	V	G	O	K	P	E	Y	M	Y	P
Y	D	L	J	S	Q	F	B	Q	M	E	C	P	M	R
X	Y	A	B	S	B	Z	Y	B	X	W	N	L	D	D
N	K	S	Q	F	D	E	T	D	V	I	I	U	F
O	E	K	M	V	T	N	U	N	D	F	A	S	C	R
V	E	R	W	Z	R	A	H	A	D	I	O	T	K	D
I	N	P	E	P	C	U	O	K	Z	G	J	E	D	F
R	J	J	D	O	B	B	M	C	I	M	L	N	H	K
E	E	L	S	R	F	T	D	T	A	H	M	P	X
A	I	W	A	I	K	O	B	X	F	I	K	Q	I	V
D	Y	V	Q	N	G	K	H	U	C	K	Y	I	G	V
F	P	Z	K	G	X	O	M	F	K	I	W	V	L	G

 Write the words. Then find them in the puzzle.

1 _____

2 _____

3 _____

4 _____

UNIT 4

The Class Rules

Teacher's Book p.99

Can you eat in English class?
Can you sleep in English class?

Ms. Parker is in the class. Where is she? She is in front of the students. She tells them the class rules. The students can read and listen. They can write and speak. But they can't eat, sleep, or sing. They can't run. Brad raises his hand. He asks, "Can I close the windows? I'm cold now."

New Words

eat

sleep

speak

raise

Part A. Spell the Words

1.

_at

(A)   e

(B)   a

(C)   i

2.

(A)   slip

(B)   sleep

(C)   sheep

Part B. Situational Writing

3.

Brad _____ his hand.

(A)   hides

(B)   raises

(C)   closes

4.

Students! Please do not _____.

(A)   run

(B)   study

(C)   listen

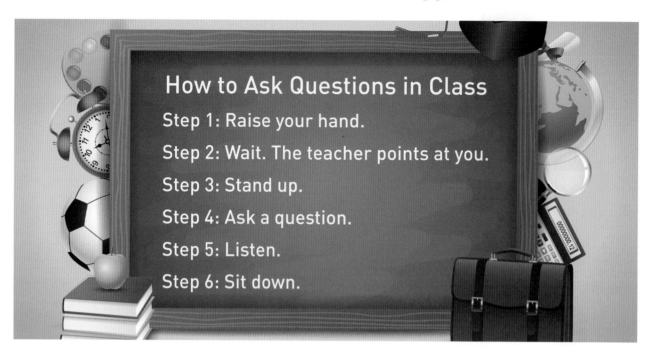

How to Ask Questions in Class

Step 1: Raise your hand.

Step 2: Wait. The teacher points at you.

Step 3: Stand up.

Step 4: Ask a question.

Step 5: Listen.

Step 6: Sit down.

5. What is NOT in a class rule?

(A) Sit down.

(B) Go to the board.

(C) Raise your hand.

6. Choose the best picture for step 3.

(A)   (B)   (C)

Part D. General Reading and Retelling

> Ms. Parker is in the class. Where is she? She is in front of the students. She tells them the class rules. The students can read and listen. They can write and speak. But they can't eat, sleep, or sing. They can't run. Brad raises his hand. He asks, "Can I close the windows? I'm cold now."

7. What is the best title?

   (A) Noisy Students
   (B) The Classroom Rules
   (C) Ms. Parker's Vacation

8. Where is Ms. Parker?

   (A) at home
   (B) in the class
   (C) under a desk

9. What can students NOT do in the class?

   (A) sleep
   (B) study
   (C) speak

10. What does Brad do?

   (A) open a door
   (B) ask a question
   (C) close a window

Listen and write.

The Class Rules

Ms. Parker is in the class. Where is she? She is in front of the students. She tells them the class rules. The students can read and listen. They can write and ¹[   ]. But they can't ²[   ], ³[   ], or sing. They can't run. Brad ⁴[   ] his hand. He asks, "Can I close the windows? I'm cold now."

Word Bank

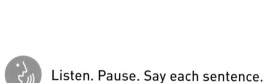

raises	slip
sleep	ett
speak	spike
raizes	eat

Listen. Pause. Say each sentence.

 MP3 PS2-4G

Writing Practice

 Write the words.

1

2 | s | | | |

3 | s | | | |

4 | r | | | |

 Write the words.

Summary

Ms. Parker tells the students the class _____s.

Brad asks a question.

Word Puzzle

M	L	K	C	D	T	O	K	D	B	A	B	V	I	Z
O	R	B	R	F	Y	A	M	I	S	O	L	V	L	B
B	W	I	K	M	H	Z	O	N	X	J	N	W	S	X
E	C	A	O	F	D	M	Z	B	O	M	S	N	O	I
Z	L	I	M	T	M	X	F	Q	B	R	K	L	T	N
P	N	V	E	L	F	W	Z	U	N	S	P	A	D	O
G	C	Q	F	J	U	K	A	E	P	D	U	H	U	C
W	O	U	L	A	B	Y	Q	U	M	L	T	D	N	I
H	Y	D	S	E	V	Q	G	W	L	Q	P	J	A	F
G	D	I	S	D	Y	R	Q	J	X	A	O	Z	V	Q
Y	W	Z	Q	S	L	O	J	P	Z	R	N	Q	G	H
D	Q	D	D	L	J	R	H	T	A	A	U	R	S	E
H	Z	M	N	E	V	C	I	L	Z	I	N	T	T	J
W	V	S	P	E	A	K	Y	A	B	S	O	A	N	M
U	U	O	X	P	P	K	C	F	M	E	A	T	D	G

 Write the words. Then find them in the puzzle.

1 _____ 2 _____ 3 _____ 4 _____

Match the pictures to the correct words.

 Teacher's Book p.102

art

class

draw

eat

eraser

listen

pencil

raise

read

sing

sleep

speak

stand

study

teacher

write

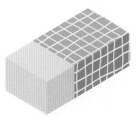

CHAPTER 2

My Day at School

UNIT 5   **Josef's Morning**   45

UNIT 6   **A School Festival**   53

UNIT 7   **A Busy Year**   61

UNIT 8   **Four Seasons**   69

CHAPTER REVIEW   77

UNIT 5

 Teacher's Book p.103

Josef's Morning

What classes do you have today?

Josef wakes up at 7 o'clock. He washes his face and takes a shower. He eats breakfast. At 7:30, he leaves home. He arrives at school at 8 o'clock. The class starts at 8:20. Today's first class is science. Now Josef is in history class. His break is at 11 o'clock.

New Words

wake up

take a shower

arrive

leave

Part A. Spell the Words

1.

_ake up

(A)   u

(B)   y

(C)   w

2.

(A)   leave

(B)   laeve

(C)   veale

Part B. Situational Writing

3.

Josef goes to _____ at 8 o'clock.

(A)   school

(B)   the beach

(C)   the mountain

4.

Josef first studies _____.

(A)   history

(B)   Korean

(C)   science

Margo's Morning

9:00	wake up
9:05	take a shower
9:30	breakfast
9:50	pack her bag
10:00	leave home

5.   When does Margo take a shower?

(A) 9:00

(B) 9:05

(C) 9:30

6.   What does Margo do at 9:50?

(A) wakes up

(B) eats breakfast

(C) packs a bag

Part D. General Reading and Retelling

Josef wakes up at 7 o'clock. He washes his face and takes a shower. He eats breakfast. At 7:30, he leaves home. He arrives at school at 8 o'clock. The class starts at 8:20. Today's first class is science. Now Josef is in history class. His break is at 11 o'clock.

7. When does Josef leave home?

   (A) at 7 o'clock
   (B) at 7:30
   (C) at 8 o'clock

8. When does Josef take a break?

   (A) at 10 o'clock
   (B) at 11 o'clock
   (C) at 12 o'clock

9. What does Josef NOT do at home?

   (A) feed his dog
   (B) take a shower
   (C) wash his face

10. What does Josef study today?

   (A) music
   (B) history
   (C) English

Listening Practice

 Listen and write.

  MP3 PS2-5

Josef's Morning

Josef ¹ _____ at 7 o'clock. He washes his face and takes a ² _____. He eats breakfast. At 7:30, he ³ _____ home. He ⁴ _____ at school at 8 o'clock. The class starts at 8:20. Today's first class is science. Now Josef is in history class. His break is at 11 o'clock.

Word Bank

shower	shawer
wakesup	wakes up
leaves	arrives
alives	lives

 Listen. Pause. Say each sentence.

  MP3 PS2-5G

Writing Practice

 Write the words.

1

| w | | | | u | |

2

| t | | | | a | | | | e | r |

3

| a | | | | |

4

| | | | e |

 Write the words.

Summary

Josef wakes up at 7:00 in the _____. After he

eats breakfast, he arrives at school at 8 o'clock and goes to

class.

N	X	E	W	V	Y	H	D	F	A	L	T	C	X	H
H	Z	W	K	I	T	E	O	I	X	Q	E	C	R	B
E	U	I	G	C	P	N	M	W	A	K	E	U	P	L
I	J	Q	J	I	C	S	D	D	T	R	G	E	W	B
T	I	M	Z	T	R	N	N	K	I	Y	J	G	M	T
X	U	S	H	T	X	M	P	L	Q	T	V	C	L	M
T	Y	H	T	A	K	E	A	S	H	O	W	E	R	Y
C	N	B	V	E	R	J	E	M	C	J	N	M	P	W
X	D	X	N	R	F	L	E	A	V	E	T	I	O	Q
S	Y	D	J	P	T	I	N	Y	Y	O	B	U	I	H
D	Y	G	N	A	R	B	M	C	R	I	O	D	H	Z
V	A	R	R	I	V	E	U	E	C	A	C	X	Q	U
E	M	B	T	P	Y	D	D	N	J	R	M	E	C	J
Y	Y	N	E	H	A	X	F	Z	X	V	O	Z	S	C
Q	G	S	N	K	K	Z	I	A	Q	T	Q	T	J	H

Write the words. Then find them in the puzzle.

1 _____

2 _____

3 _____

4 _____

UNIT 6

A School Festival

Teacher's Book
p.106

Think about a school festival.
What do you do?

This week is a school festival. There are many special days. Students are excited. Today is Monday. It is Book Club day. Tomorrow is Sports Day. Wednesday is Science Day. A field trip is on Thursday. Friday is a dance party! This week is a happy week.

New Words

Monday

Tuesday

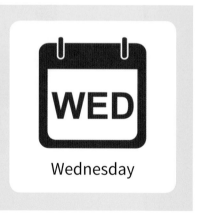

Wednesday

Thursday

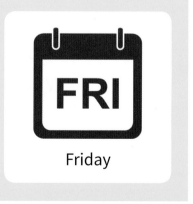

Friday

Part A. Spell the Words

1.

_estival

(A)   f

(B)   p

(C)   b

2.

(A)   porsts

(B)   sports

(C)   soprts

Part B. Situational Writing

3.

Monday is _____ Club day.

(A)   Book

(B)   Music

(C)   Dance

4.

On Thursday, students go on a _____.

(A)   trip

(B)   boat

(C)   river

Part C. Practical Reading and Retelling

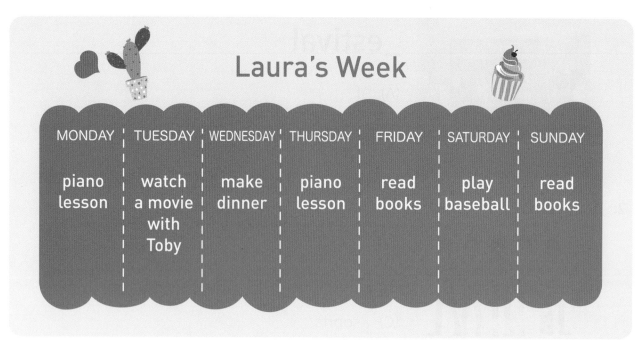

Laura's Week

MONDAY	TUESDAY	WEDNESDAY	THURSDAY	FRIDAY	SATURDAY	SUNDAY
piano lesson	watch a movie with Toby	make dinner	piano lesson	read books	play baseball	read books

5. What does Laura do on Friday?

    (A) watch a movie

    (B) play the piano

    (C) read books

6. When does Laura make dinner?

    (A) on Monday

    (B) on Tuesday

    (C) on Wednesday

Part D. General Reading and Retelling

This week is a school festival. There are many special days. Students are excited. Today is Monday. It is Book Club day. Tomorrow is Sports Day. Wednesday is Science Day. A field trip is on Thursday. Friday is a dance party! This week is a happy week.

7. What is the best title?

(A) Science Fair
(B) Book Festival
(C) School Festival Week

8. What is special this week?

(A) a final exam
(B) a new teacher
(C) a school festival

9. What is Tuesday?

(A) Book Day
(B) Sports Day
(C) Science Day

10. When is there a party?

(A) on Wednesday
(B) on Thursday
(C) on Friday

Listening Practice

 Listen and write.

  MP3 PS2-6

A School Festival

This week is a school festival. There are many special days.

Students are excited. Today is ¹ [   ]. It is Book Club

day. Tomorrow is Sports Day. ² [   ] is Science Day.

A field trip is on ³ [   ]. ⁴ [   ] is a dance

party! This week is a happy week.

Word Bank

Thursday	fly day
Wednesday	Friday
wednesday	Monday
Thirstday	monday

 Listen. Pause. Say each sentence.

  MP3 PS2-6G

Writing Practice

 Write the words.

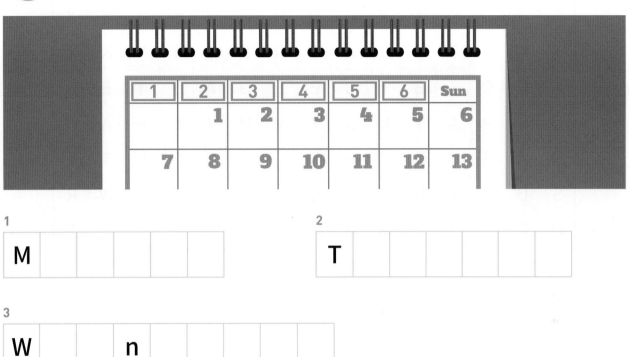

1

M				

2

T					

3

W		n				

4

T						

5

F					

6

S		t				

 Write the words.

Summary

It is school _____ week. There are many special

days. Students are excited.

S	J	D	S	T	P	U	B	H	W	Y	W	K	Y	Y
T	A	Y	T	J	O	A	E	N	E	G	T	Y	N	I
H	D	C	Z	B	T	U	E	S	D	A	Y	Y	E	H
U	Q	R	A	I	N	J	Y	V	N	V	E	F	A	W
R	A	G	Q	X	V	P	X	L	E	Q	B	R	T	T
S	G	O	I	B	K	S	E	N	S	H	F	I	W	R
D	Z	T	R	F	M	K	H	P	D	B	L	D	S	T
A	C	E	R	A	I	F	N	M	A	L	X	A	W	G
Y	U	D	C	M	O	N	D	A	Y	A	Z	Y	I	Q
R	J	V	H	O	P	L	N	G	E	Z	F	K	X	O
J	S	E	U	J	R	F	C	N	M	R	T	Z	L	B
I	Z	T	E	R	Q	G	I	B	S	S	P	L	U	N
I	Y	M	J	B	Q	N	M	N	I	H	A	J	P	V
C	Y	R	U	L	O	H	J	D	Z	V	K	T	C	H
E	O	M	Y	L	E	O	O	Z	S	B	P	P	Z	E

 Write the words. Then find them in the puzzle.

1 _____ 2 _____ 3 _____ 4 _____ 5 _____

UNIT 7

A Busy Year

Teacher's Book p.109

When is your summer vacation?
When do you start school?

Marta is busy this year. She starts school in January. She swims in February. In March, she has a short break. She studies hard in April, May, and June. July and August are vacation months. School starts again in September. In October, Marta's family goes to Paris. November and December are cold. Marta reads books then.

New Words

break

vacation

cold

swim

Part A. Spell the Words

1.

_old

(A) k

(B) c

(C) t

2.

(A) swim

(B) siwm

(C) smiw

Part B. Situational Writing

3.

In May, Marta _____ hard.

(A) runs

(B) cooks

(C) studies

4.

Their _____ is in August.

(A) test

(B) exam

(C) vacation

UNIT 7 A Busy Year

DECEMBER 2019

SUN	MON	TUE	WED	THU	FRI	SAT
1	2	3	4	⑤ exam	6	7
8	9	10	11	⑫ sister's birthday	13	14
15	16	17	18	19	⑳	21 winter vacation
22	23	24	㉕ Christmas	26	27	28 starts
29	30	31				

5. When is the sister's birthday?

(A) December 5th

(B) December 12th

(C) December 25th

6. What starts on December 20th?

(A) an exam

(B) Christmas

(C) winter vacation

Part D. General Reading and Retelling

Marta is busy this year. She starts school in January. She swims in February. In March, she has a short break. She studies hard in April, May, and June. July and August are vacation months. School starts again in September. In October, Marta's family goes to Paris. November and December are cold. Marta reads books then.

7. How many months are in one year?

    (A) 11
    (B) 12
    (C) 13

8. Which month comes after May?

    (A) March
    (B) April
    (C) June

9. When does Marta swim?

    (A) February
    (B) September
    (C) December

10. When does Marta have a vacation?

    (A) June and July
    (B) July and August
    (C) June, July, and August

Listening Practice

 Listen and write.

  MP3 PS2-7

A Busy Year

Marta is busy this year. She starts school in January. She

__1_____ in February. In March, she has a short

__2_____. She studies hard in April, May, and June.

July and August are __3_____ months. School starts

again in September. In October, Marta's family goes to

Paris. November and December are __4_____. Marta

reads books then.

Word Bank

vacation	cold
bacation	swems
break	blake
swims	kold

 Listen. Pause. Say each sentence.

 MP3 PS2-7G

Writing Practice

 Write the words.

1
b			

2
	a					n

3
	o	

4
		i	

 Write the words.

Summary

Marta is _____ this year. She has school and

swimming lessons. She goes to France and read books.

B	U	B	S	C	J	H	H	W	T	B	D	C	Q	B
P	O	L	C	O	L	D	K	H	B	R	E	A	K	S
P	K	I	O	J	M	M	G	B	K	N	Q	O	Y	W
D	R	I	E	L	A	B	F	I	V	N	A	Y	J	E
C	B	T	V	I	G	X	H	T	Q	W	W	N	Y	J
T	M	V	H	C	T	G	W	O	U	M	Q	V	V	C
S	S	W	I	M	E	T	T	U	W	O	R	S	V	C
X	P	F	A	M	W	T	S	N	M	Y	P	D	A	C
H	Y	J	S	N	N	Y	J	H	L	F	Q	F	C	P
F	C	O	T	T	F	G	V	Q	C	X	F	F	A	E
Q	I	B	D	N	B	W	P	S	Z	N	L	D	T	L
N	X	Q	N	L	Y	A	U	G	Z	T	O	A	I	W
N	J	E	Z	H	F	E	L	P	Z	N	R	E	O	L
B	D	S	K	L	R	E	I	Z	X	E	K	H	N	B
K	C	X	O	W	H	W	I	M	L	T	U	N	L	S

 Write the words. Then find them in the puzzle.

1 _____ 2 _____ 3 _____ 4 _____

UNIT 8

Four Seasons

Teacher's Book p.112

What is your favorite season?
Why do you like it?

Parkland has four seasons. In spring, it is sunny and warm. The weather is great for picnics. And there are also many flowers. In summer, it is hot. People go swimming. The fall is cool. The sky is clear in fall. Winter in Parkland is cloudy. And winter is cold. People wear big hats in winter.

New Words

spring

summer

fall

winter

Part A. Spell the Words

1.

   # fa_l

   (A) l

   (B) r

   (C) s

2.

   (A) flyers

   (B) flowers

   (C) showers

Part B. Situational Writing

3.

   There are four _____ in Parkland.

   (A) trees

   (B) clouds

   (C) seasons

4.

   Parkland is _____ in winter.

   (A) warm

   (B) sunny

   (C) cloudy

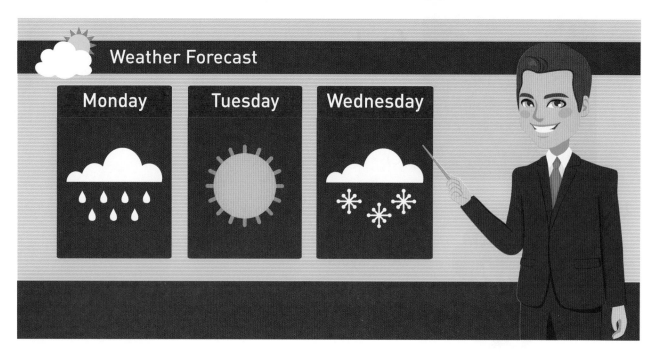

5. What is Tuesday's weather?

   (A) sunny

   (B) snowy

   (C) stormy

6. When is it rainy?

   (A) on Monday

   (B) on Tuesday

   (C) on Wednesday

Part D. General Reading and Retelling

Parkland has four seasons. In spring, it is sunny and warm. The weather is great for picnics. And there are also many flowers. In summer, it is hot. People go swimming. The fall is cool. The sky is clear in fall. Winter in Parkland is cloudy. And winter is cold. People wear big hats in winter.

7. How is Parkland in spring?

   (A) foggy
   (B) cloudy
   (C) sunny

8. When is the sky clear in Parkland?

   (A) in spring
   (B) in summer
   (C) in fall

9. When do Parkland people go swimming?

   (A) in spring
   (B) in summer
   (C) in fall

10. What do Parkland people wear in winter?

   (A) big hats
   (B) swimsuits
   (C) long scarves

Listening Practice

 Listen and write.

  MP3 PS2-8

Four Seasons

Parkland has four seasons. In ¹ _____, it is sunny and warm. The weather is great for picnics. And there are also many flowers. In ² _____, it is hot. People go swimming. The ³ _____ is cool. The sky is clear in fall. ⁴ _____ in Parkland is cloudy. And winter is cold. People wear big hats in winter.

Word Bank

pall	spring
sumer	summer
fall	winter
spling	uinter

 Listen. Pause. Say each sentence.

  MP3 PS2-8G

Writing Practice ────────────────

 Write the words.

1

s				

2

				r

3

			l

4

	i			

 Write the words.

Summary
────────────────────────────────

Parkland has four _____. It is warm in spring.

It is hot in summer. It is cool in fall. It is cold in winter.

M	Z	O	Q	R	Y	P	P	Z	T	D	T	G	C	M
E	G	G	D	K	D	J	U	C	D	C	F	S	H	T
W	S	D	F	Y	A	N	T	Z	A	G	K	U	Y	V
B	P	R	C	V	I	E	E	O	W	J	J	M	O	W
C	R	X	V	V	K	K	G	E	P	S	O	M	L	I
W	I	V	J	L	B	Q	U	M	Y	C	X	E	X	N
E	N	U	C	C	C	R	X	H	A	B	W	R	L	T
U	G	E	G	G	H	B	E	O	J	B	A	Y	O	E
K	X	V	G	K	R	G	Z	H	V	N	D	Y	E	R
F	I	O	A	P	U	S	X	C	X	E	T	J	K
G	Z	L	U	B	L	X	S	Q	Q	R	H	P	K	F
J	H	S	I	R	R	M	S	L	L	B	L	L	M	L
G	Q	A	E	Q	E	L	V	F	J	Y	Z	A	Q	O
L	E	P	S	D	Q	H	B	P	Y	Z	Y	D	A	Q
E	N	L	C	T	N	F	V	W	F	J	F	A	L	L

Write the words. Then find them in the puzzle.

1 _____   2 _____   3 _____   4 _____

CHAPTER REVIEW

Match the pictures to the correct words.

Teacher's Book
p.115

arrive

break

cold

fall

Friday

leave

Monday

spring

summer

swim

take a shower

Thursday

Tuesday

vacation

wake up

Wednesday

winter

WED

THU

CHAPTER 3

At School

UNIT 9   **Olaf's Day**   79

UNIT 10   **Shopping with Your Family**   87

UNIT 11   **Henry and His Bike**   95

UNIT 12   **Tennis and Table Tennis**   103

CHAPTER REVIEW   111

Teacher's Book
p.116

UNIT 9

Olaf's Day

Look at Olaf. Think.
How is he feeling today?

Today is Olaf's test day. Olaf takes the test. His score is great! Olaf is happy. After school, Olaf plays baseball. His team loses the game! And Olaf loses his bat. He is sad. He goes home. He is tired now. Then, Olaf plays with his dog. He feels happy.

New Words

baseball

lose

bat

tired

Part A. Spell the Words

1.

tir_d

(A) e

(B) i

(C) a

2.

_ad

(A) s

(B) d

(C) h

Part B. Situational Writing

3.

Olaf is _____.

(A) sad

(B) happy

(C) angry

4.

His team _____.

(A) wins

(B) loses

(C) jumps

5. How does the student feel?

   (A) He is excited.

   (B) He is happy.

   (C) He feels sleepy.

6. How does the teacher feel?

   (A) She is angry.

   (B) She feels hungry.

   (C) She is excited.

Part D. General Reading and Retelling

Today is Olaf's test day. Olaf takes the test. His score is great! Olaf is happy. After school, Olaf plays baseball. His team loses the game! And Olaf loses his bat. He is sad. He goes home. He is tired now. Then, Olaf plays with his dog. He feels happy.

7. What is the best title?

(A) Olaf's Day
(B) Olaf's Test
(C) Olaf's Home

8. What does Olaf play after school?

(A) soccer
(B) baseball
(C) basketball

9. How does Olaf feel after his game?

(A) sad
(B) sleepy
(C) hungry

10. Where does Olaf's dog play?

(A) at home
(B) at school
(C) at the park

Listening Practice

 Listen and write.

  MP3 PS2-9

Olaf's Day

Today is Olaf's test day. Olaf takes the test. His score is

great! Olaf is happy. After school, Olaf plays [¹]_____.

His team [²]_____ the game! And Olaf loses his

[³]_____. He is sad. He goes home. He is [⁴]_____

now. Then, Olaf plays with his dog. He feels happy.

Word Bank

loses	beseball
baseball	tird
bat	tired
loozes	vat

 Listen. Pause. Say each sentence.

 MP3 PS2-9G

Writing Practice

 Write the words.

1

b						l

2

			e

3

4

t			

 Write the words.

Summary

Today, Olaf is _____. Then he is sad. Then he is happy again!

E	M	U	C	O	J	B	A	S	E	B	A	L	L	K
T	I	R	E	D	Q	P	K	Z	U	N	Q	X	C	W
P	Q	X	X	I	Y	T	U	O	Q	F	U	L	F	Y
J	S	B	U	C	E	G	F	S	M	K	A	U	D	T
F	U	W	O	H	E	J	R	R	C	Z	C	K	S	T
W	W	H	N	B	L	B	W	N	Y	V	R	I	V	D
R	J	A	S	Y	Y	E	O	K	L	H	B	K	V	V
X	O	R	T	F	B	M	B	J	Q	V	O	P	K	N
G	V	J	G	O	A	C	K	K	O	M	A	M	E	O
M	A	Q	I	S	H	T	I	Y	X	O	T	G	D	N
S	H	L	F	S	P	F	B	A	T	H	I	P	O	B
S	D	N	R	Z	V	Y	X	L	B	O	B	L	R	D
K	G	U	I	Q	G	V	O	J	H	L	H	O	O	K
G	R	U	F	X	G	S	O	P	A	R	E	S	W	J
R	N	J	P	N	Q	A	Y	K	W	G	G	E	Z	U

🔍 Write the words. Then find them in the puzzle.

1 _____   2 _____   3 _____   4 _____

UNIT 10

Shopping with Your Family

 Teacher's Book p.119

Where are they? What are they doing?

It is Sunday. Dina's family goes shopping. Her father buys a glass. It is for his orange juice. Dina's mother and brother buy umbrellas. What color is her mother's umbrella? It is blue. It has white dots. What color is her brother's umbrella? It is red. It has yellow lines. Dina buys a hat. It is her first hat.

New Words

glass

umbrella

hat

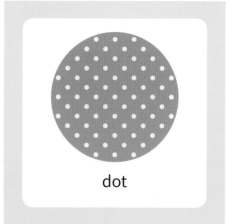

dot

1.

_mbrella

(A)   a

(B)   e

(C)   u

2.

(A)   sitting

(B)   sleeping

(C)   shopping

Part B. Situational Writing

3.

I need a _____.

(A)   glass

(B)   dress

(C)   glove

4.

It is a _____ umbrella.

(A)   red

(B)   blue

(C)   white

UNIT 10   Shopping with Your Family

5. What is in the picture?

    (A) a mirror
    (B) scissors
    (C) an umbrella

6. Guess. Whose bag is it?

    (A) a doctor's bag
    (B) a student's bag
    (C) a musician's bag

Part D. General Reading and Retelling

It is Sunday. Dina's family goes shopping. Her father buys a glass. It is for his orange juice. Dina's mother and brother buy umbrellas. What color is her mother's umbrella? It is blue. It has white dots. What color is her brother's umbrella? It is red. It has yellow lines. Dina buys a hat. It is her first hat.

7. What is the best title?

   (A) Family Dinner
   (B) Family Clothing
   (C) Family Shopping

8. Who drinks orange juice?

   (A) Dina
   (B) Dina's father
   (C) Dina's mother

9. What does Dina's brother buy?

   (A) a yellow cup
   (B) a red umbrella
   (C) a blue umbrella

10. What is true about Dina?

   (A) She has many hats.
   (B) She buys a new hat.
   (C) She shops on Saturday.

Listening Practice

 Listen and write.

  MP3 PS2-10

Shopping with Your Family

It is Sunday. Dina's family goes shopping. Her father buys a ¹ _____ . It is for his orange juice. Dina's mother and brother buy ² _____ . What color is her mother's umbrella? It is blue. It has white ³ _____ . What color is her brother's umbrella? It is red. It has yellow lines. Dina buys a ⁴ _____ . It is her first hat.

Word Bank

hatt	umbrelas
grass	umbrellas
dats	hat
glass	dots

 Listen. Pause. Say each sentence.

  MP3 PS2-10G

Writing Practice

 Write the words.

1
| | | | | s |

2
| | m | | | | | a |

3
| | | |

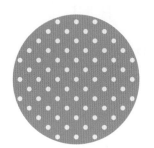

4
| | | |

 Write the words.

Summary

Dina's family goes _____ on Sunday. They buy a glass, umbrellas, and a hat.

Word Puzzle

G	P	R	R	D	H	R	H	N	K	M	I	M	M	Q
L	Z	E	O	A	A	A	P	G	N	G	N	U	G	Y
U	X	P	F	L	H	J	Q	W	K	L	W	J	K	T
V	R	G	E	L	H	S	U	Q	S	A	K	N	G	Z
F	S	Z	O	L	V	Z	A	H	O	S	L	F	F	C
O	A	J	R	O	M	A	Y	Z	N	S	B	Y	B	G
R	U	T	Q	D	M	R	X	W	Z	G	O	K	E	F
R	O	E	U	I	W	B	U	U	C	Z	G	D	D	U
G	J	R	N	B	G	F	X	B	W	J	A	O	C	M
I	F	R	T	Z	K	C	Q	U	Q	R	B	T	J	B
Y	H	A	T	H	E	H	S	D	M	U	A	Y	C	R
N	V	D	C	C	S	K	Z	I	F	U	A	W	P	E
Y	Y	K	M	X	O	D	W	V	X	O	C	W	S	L
M	L	F	M	F	D	N	Y	N	S	T	H	B	P	L
I	H	W	V	I	K	T	Z	D	M	L	O	B	W	A

 Write the words. Then find them in the puzzle.

         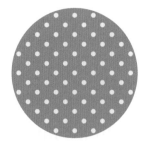

1 _____   2 _____   3 _____   4 _____

UNIT 11

Teacher's Book p.122

Henry and His Bike

How do you go to school?

Henry goes to school. How does he go there? He rides his bike. He likes his bike. But one wheel breaks. So today he takes the bus. After school, Henry's father comes. He drives a car. He gets Henry. They go to a shop. A worker fixes the bike. Henry gets a new wheel. He rides his bike home.

New Words

bike

bus

car

wheel

Part A. Spell the Words

1.

__eel

(A)   wh

(B)   ch

(C)   th

2.

(A)   bike

(B)   mike

(C)   hike

Part B. Situational Writing

3.

Henry's father can drive a _____.

(A)   car

(B)   train

(C)   boat

4.

The worker _____ Henry's bike.

(A)   fixes

(B)   rides

(C)   breaks

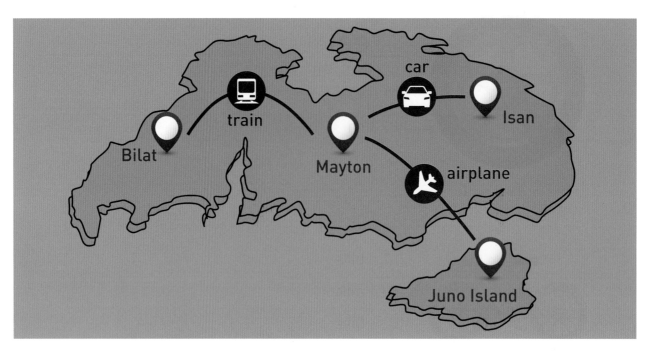

5. How do you go from Mayton to Bilat?

    (A) by train
    (B) by car
    (C) by airplane

6. Take an airplane from Mayton. Where can you go?

    (A) to Isan
    (B) to Bilat
    (C) to Juno Island

Part D. General Reading and Retelling

Henry goes to school. How does he go there? He rides his bike. He likes his bike. But one wheel breaks. So today he takes the bus. After school, Henry's father comes. He drives a car. He gets Henry. They go to a shop. A worker fixes the bike. Henry gets a new wheel. He rides his bike home.

7. What happens to Henry's bike?

   (A) It gets wet.
   (B) Henry paints it.
   (C) The wheel breaks.

8. How does Henry go to school today?

   (A) by bus
   (B) by car
   (C) by bike

9. How does Henry get home?

   (A) on foot
   (B) by taxi
   (C) by bicycle

10. What is true?

   (A) Henry likes his bike.
   (B) Henry learns to drive.
   (C) Henry gets a new bike.

UNIT 11 Henry and His Bike

Listen and write.

 MP3 PS2-11

Henry and His Bike

Henry goes to school. How does he go there? He rides his ¹ _____ . He likes his bike. But one ² _____ breaks. So today he takes the ³ _____ . After school, Henry's father comes. He drives a ⁴ _____ . He gets Henry. They go to a shop. A worker fixes the bike. Henry gets a new wheel. He rides his bike home.

Word Bank

bus	bike
vike	wheel
buss	car
we're	kar

 Listen. Pause. Say each sentence.

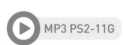 MP3 PS2-11G

Writing Practice

 Write the words.

1
b			

2

3

4
		e	

 Write the words.

Summary

Henry usually _____ his bike to school. But his
wheel breaks. Henry's dad helps him.

M	V	W	M	U	W	B	M	U	S	A	W	E	Z	F
W	F	H	S	D	R	Z	J	Z	L	B	D	L	K	E
J	N	E	Z	T	B	U	S	V	Y	G	P	B	M	S
H	M	E	K	B	I	Q	H	P	U	S	L	W	W	D
C	J	L	P	Q	K	M	Z	X	C	A	T	K	W	Q
O	I	W	M	O	E	P	V	U	E	D	X	H	C	H
Q	D	B	D	Q	J	F	E	Q	J	U	W	T	Z	K
X	B	H	Q	O	C	H	D	O	B	O	O	X	K	L
O	G	S	W	O	Y	R	U	S	R	S	B	G	W	J
T	Y	J	U	V	D	R	H	K	U	U	A	P	S	W
V	A	U	W	V	A	H	O	V	S	Z	L	R	P	Y
T	C	O	U	C	Z	I	E	L	M	X	C	A	R	M
W	C	T	N	V	S	S	I	Z	C	M	W	H	I	P
D	X	B	G	K	C	O	Z	U	B	R	T	A	F	O
Z	U	Z	Z	U	T	L	D	V	V	F	L	K	E	E

🔍 Write the words. Then find them in the puzzle.

1 _____   2 _____   3 _____   4 _____

UNIT 12

 Teacher's Book p.126

Tennis and Table Tennis

Can you play tennis?
What is your favorite sport?

What is tennis? There are two players. Or there are four players. The players hit a ball. What is in their hand? There is a racket. Where does the ball go? It goes across the net. It touches the ground. What is table tennis? It is like tennis. But there is a table. And the ball is small. The ball touches the table.

New Words

tennis

ball

racket

table tennis

Part A. Spell the Words

1.

ra__et

(A)   sh

(B)   ck

(C)   wh

2.

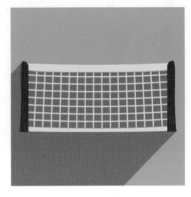

(A)   net

(B)   etn

(C)   ten

Part B. Situational Writing

3.

It is a yellow _____.

(A)   ball

(B)   net

(C)   racket

4.

The players have a blue _____.

(A)   net

(B)   ball

(C)   table

Part C. Practical Reading and Retelling

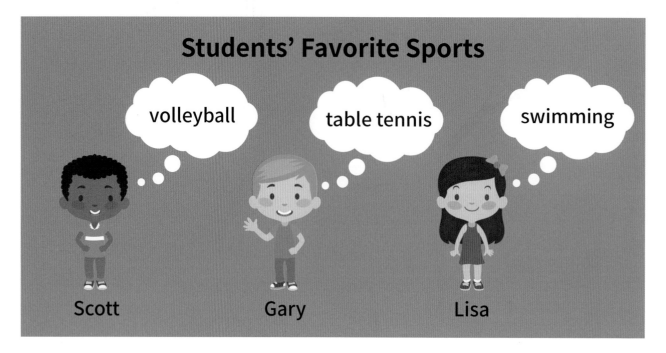

Students' Favorite Sports

volleyball · table tennis · swimming

Scott · Gary · Lisa

5. What is Lisa's favorite sport?

(A)   (B)   (C)

6. Whose favorite sport is table tennis?

(A) Scott

(B) Gary

(C) Lisa

Part D. General Reading and Retelling

What is tennis? There are two players. Or there are four players. The players hit a ball. What is in their hand? There is a racket. Where does the ball go? It goes across the net. It touches the ground. What is table tennis? It is like tennis. But there is a table. And the ball is small. The ball touches the table.

7. Which is for tennis?

(A) a bat
(B) a racket
(C) a baseball

8. What do tennis players do?

(A) hit a ball
(B) kick a ball
(C) catch a ball

9. What is true about table tennis?

(A) The ball is big.
(B) There is no ball.
(C) The ball is small.

10. What is wrong in the picture?

(A) The players have rackets.
(B) There are too many players.
(C) The ball goes across the net.

Listening Practice

 Listen and write.

  MP3 PS2-12

Tennis and Table Tennis

What is ¹_____? There are two players. Or there are four players. The players hit a ²_____. What is in their hand? There is a ³_____. Where does the ball go? It goes across the net. It touches the ground. What is ⁴_____ tennis? It is like tennis. But there is a table. And the ball is small. The ball touches the table.

Word Bank

tenis	ball
table	boll
raket	racket
tavel	tennis

 Listen. Pause. Say each sentence.

  MP3 PS2-12G

Writing Practice

 Write the words.

1

| t | | | | | |

2

| b | | | |

3

| | | | | | t |

4

| t | | | | | t | | | | s |

 Write the words.

Summary

_____ players hit a ball with a racket. Table

tennis is like tennis with a table.

Word Puzzle

T	W	G	U	V	P	G	O	F	U	J	F	Z	W	J
K	G	B	P	P	Y	T	U	F	O	K	M	H	T	K
C	Z	B	S	O	V	L	Y	T	B	O	F	B	A	L
N	O	A	P	Z	R	A	X	D	Q	G	D	P	B	Y
P	J	L	O	W	D	H	P	I	Z	K	O	T	L	E
T	I	L	O	Z	T	G	B	Y	Q	Y	G	L	E	D
W	T	K	K	U	C	X	H	F	W	V	M	N	T	X
D	F	H	Y	Q	D	Q	R	S	R	A	C	K	E	T
V	C	X	S	Y	J	J	Z	W	P	R	X	W	N	A
G	G	X	G	C	A	P	O	I	S	Y	Z	U	N	E
H	D	A	E	S	T	X	A	G	X	I	G	X	I	M
R	T	F	H	U	P	F	A	J	U	C	L	D	S	Z
L	T	J	T	O	N	H	Z	O	B	U	V	O	U	N
T	T	E	N	N	I	S	R	E	N	T	K	R	R	M
J	E	F	B	K	S	M	Q	F	H	Q	N	P	C	M

🔍 Write the words. Then find them in the puzzle.

1 _____   2 _____   3 _____   4 _____

CHAPTER REVIEW

 Match the pictures to the correct words.

ball

baseball

bat

bike

bus

car

dot

glass

hat

lose

racket

table tennis

(tennis)

tired

umbrella

wheel

ANSWERS

CHAPTER 1 | In My Classroom — p.10

UNIT 1 · PS2-1 · p.11

	1	2	3	4	5	6	7	8	9	10
⏱	1 (A)	2 (C)	3 (A)	4 (B)	5 (A)	6 (A)	7 (C)	8 (B)	9 (A)	10 (B)
🎧	1 teacher		2 art		3 draws		4 class			
✏	1 art		2 draw		3 teacher		4 class		📄 art	
✳	1 art		2 draw		3 teacher		4 class			

UNIT 2 · PS2-2 · p.19

	1	2	3	4	5	6	7	8	9	10
⏱	1 (A)	2 (B)	3 (B)	4 (B)	5 (B)	6 (C)	7 (B)	8 (B)	9 (C)	10 (C)
🎧	1 stands		2 pencil		3 eraser		4 writes			
✏	1 stand		2 write		3 eraser		4 pencil		📄 math	
✳	1 stand		2 write		3 eraser		4 pencil			

UNIT 3 · PS2-3 · p.27

	1	2	3	4	5	6	7	8	9	10
⏱	1 (B)	2 (B)	3 (C)	4 (C)	5 (B)	6 (C)	7 (C)	8 (A)	9 (C)	10 (B)
🎧	1 studies		2 reads		3 listens		4 sings			
✏	1 read		2 listen		3 sing		4 study		📄 study	
✳	1 read		2 listen		3 sing		4 study			

UNIT 4 · PS2-4 · p.35

	1	2	3	4	5	6	7	8	9	10
⏱	1 (A)	2 (B)	3 (B)	4 (A)	5 (B)	6 (C)	7 (B)	8 (B)	9 (A)	10 (B)
🎧	1 speak		2 eat		3 sleep		4 raises			
✏	1 eat		2 sleep		3 speak		4 raise		📄 rule	
✳	1 eat		2 sleep		3 speak		4 raise			

CHAPTER 2 | My Day at School — p.44

UNIT 5 · PS2-5 · p.45

	1	2	3	4	5	6	7	8	9	10
⏱	1 (C)	2 (A)	3 (A)	4 (C)	5 (B)	6 (C)	7 (B)	8 (B)	9 (A)	10 (B)
🎧	1 wakes up		2 shower		3 leaves		4 arrives			
✏	1 wake up		2 take a shower		3 arrive		4 leave		📄 morning	
✳	1 wake up		2 take a shower		3 arrive		4 leave			

UNIT 6 · PS2-6 · p.53

	1	2	3	4	5	6	7	8	9	10
⏱	1 (A)	2 (B)	3 (A)	4 (A)	5 (C)	6 (C)	7 (C)	8 (C)	9 (B)	10 (C)
🎧	1 Monday		2 Wednesday		3 Thursday		4 Friday			
✏	1 Monday	2 Tuesday	3 Wednesday	4 Thursday	5 Friday		6 Saturday		📄 festival	
✳	1 Monday	2 Tuesday	3 Wednesday	4 Thursday	5 Friday					

UNIT 7 · PS2-7 · p.61

	1	2	3	4	5	6	7	8	9	10
⏱	1 (B)	2 (A)	3 (C)	4 (C)	5 (B)	6 (C)	7 (B)	8 (C)	9 (A)	10 (B)
🎧	1 swims		2 break		3 vacation		4 cold			
✏	1 break		2 vacation		3 cold		4 swim		📄 busy	
✳	1 break		2 vacation		3 cold		4 swim			

UNIT 8 · PS2-8 · p.69

	1	2	3	4	5	6	7	8	9	10
⏱	1 (A)	2 (B)	3 (C)	4 (C)	5 (A)	6 (A)	7 (C)	8 (C)	9 (B)	10 (A)
🎧	1 spring		2 summer		3 fall		4 Winter			
✏	1 spring		2 summer		3 fall		4 winter		📄 seasons	
✳	1 spring		2 summer		3 fall		4 winter			

CHAPTER 3 | At School — p.78

UNIT 9 · PS2-9 · p.79

	1	2	3	4	5	6	7	8	9	10
⏱	1 (A)	2 (A)	3 (B)	4 (B)	5 (C)	6 (A)	7 (A)	8 (B)	9 (A)	10 (A)
🎧	1 baseball		2 loses		3 bat		4 tired			
✏	1 baseball		2 lose		3 bat		4 tired		📄 happy	
✳	1 baseball		2 lose		3 bat		4 tired			

UNIT 10 · PS2-10 · p.87

	1	2	3	4	5	6	7	8	9	10
⏱	1 (C)	2 (C)	3 (A)	4 (B)	5 (B)	6 (B)	7 (C)	8 (B)	9 (B)	10 (B)
🎧	1 glass		2 umbrellas		3 dots		4 hat			
✏	1 glass		2 umbrella		3 hat		4 dot		📄 shopping	
✳	1 glass		2 umbrella		3 hat		4 dot			

UNIT 11 · PS2-11 · p.95

	1	2	3	4	5	6	7	8	9	10
⏱	1 (A)	2 (A)	3 (A)	4 (A)	5 (A)	6 (C)	7 (C)	8 (A)	9 (C)	10 (A)
🎧	1 bike		2 wheel		3 bus		4 car			
✏	1 bike		2 bus		3 car		4 wheel		📄 rides	
✳	1 bike		2 bus		3 car		4 wheel			

UNIT 12 · PS2-12 · p.103

	1	2	3	4	5	6	7	8	9	10
⏱	1 (B)	2 (A)	3 (A)	4 (C)	5 (C)	6 (B)	7 (B)	8 (A)	9 (C)	10 (B)
🎧	1 tennis		2 ball		3 racket		4 table			
✏	1 tennis		2 ball		3 racket		4 table tennis		📄 Tennis	
✳	1 tennis		2 ball		3 racket		4 table tennis			